CONTEMPORARY LIVES

ROBERT DOWNEY JR.

BLOCKBUSTER MOVIE STAR

ABDO
Publishing Company

CONTEMPORARY LIVES

ROBERT DOWNEY JR.

BLOCKBUSTER MOVIE STAR

by Stephanie Watson

CREDITS

Published by ABDO Publishing Company, PO Box 398166, Minneapolis, Minnesota 55439. Copyright © 2012 by Abdo Consulting Group, Inc. International copyrights reserved in all countries. No part of this book may be reproduced in any form without written permission from the publisher. The Essential Library™ is a trademark and logo of ABDO Publishing Company.

Printed in the United States of America,
North Mankato, Minnesota
112011
012012

 THIS BOOK CONTAINS AT LEAST 10% RECYCLED MATERIALS.

Editor: Melissa York
Copy Editor: Mari Kesselring
Series design and interior production: Emily Love
Cover production: Marie Tupy and Kelsey Oseid

Library of Congress Cataloging-in-Publication Data
Watson, Stephanie.
  Robert Downey Jr. : blockbuster movie star / by Stephanie Watson.
    p. cm. -- (Contemporary lives)
  Includes bibliographical references and index.
  ISBN 978-1-61783-322-9
  1. Downey, Robert, 1965- Juvenile literature. 2. Actors--United States--Biography--Juvenile literature. I. Title.
  PN2287.D548W38 2012
  791.4302'8092--dc23
  [B]
                          2011040471

TABLE OF CONTENTS

1   THE MAKING OF A SUPERHERO   6

2   AN UNCONVENTIONAL
    CHILDHOOD   14

3   MAKING IT AS AN ACTOR   22

4   DEEP INTO DRUGS   32

5   BAD CHOICES   38

6   BECOMING CHAPLIN   48

7   TROUBLE WITH THE LAW   60

8   EMERGING FROM THE
    DARKNESS   76

9   RECOVERY, REINVENTION,
    AND CAREER REBIRTH   86

TIMELINE   96

GET THE SCOOP   100

GLOSSARY   102

ADDITIONAL RESOURCES   104

SOURCE NOTES   106

INDEX   110

ABOUT THE AUTHOR   112

Robert Downey Jr. landed the title role in *Iron Man*.

CHAPTER 1

The Making of a Superhero

||||||||||||||||||||||||||||||||||||||||||||||||||||||||||||||||||||||||||||||||||

Superhero movies such as *Superman*, *Batman*, and *Spider-Man* are worth big money—and Hollywood knows it. A big-budget superhero film plus a few high-grossing sequels can make a studio's income soar. So when Marvel Studios decided to produce a movie about another superhero—Iron Man—its executives knew how much money was at stake. The film was such a big deal that it had an estimated budget of $140 million. Director Jon Favreau knew he'd need a very special actor to fill the lead role of Tony Stark, who became Iron Man. But who?

Robert Downey Jr. had grown up reading superhero comic books. He'd always wanted to play a caped crusader or masked avenger. He knew *Iron Man* was his chance. But by the time Favreau started casting *Iron Man*, Downey had already earned a reputation in Hollywood, and that reputation wasn't entirely good.

On the one hand, Downey had received some of the highest praise an actor can get. Reporters

WHO IS TONY STARK?

Tony Stark in *Iron Man* isn't your average superhero. He didn't get bitten by a radioactive spider, like Spider-Man, or arrive from a distant planet, like Superman. Stark was a self-made superhero.

Stark ran a multimillion-dollar arms company and lived a self-indulgent life, until he was captured by terrorists and injured by a bomb that left a piece of shrapnel dangerously close to his heart. Fortunately for him, he was imprisoned with a world-famous physicist. Together, the two men built a suit of iron. A special magnet in the suit prevented the shrapnel from reaching Stark's heart. That suit transformed Stark from a super-industrialist into a superhero.

and critics constantly referred to him as "one of the most gifted actors of his generation."[1] He'd won critical acclaim and an Oscar nomination for his spot-on portrayal of Charlie Chaplin in 1992. He'd also gotten rave reviews for his work in movies such as *The Singing Detective* (2003), *Kiss Kiss Bang Bang* (2005), and *Fur* (2006).

Yet Downey had become known as much for his off-camera troubles as for his on-camera talent. He'd struggled with drug addiction throughout the 1990s, showing up late to movie sets and behaving badly behind the scenes. After a string of very public arrests, Downey was appearing on-screen in a bright orange prison jumpsuit more often than in wardrobe. He bounced back and forth between rehab, jail, and rehab again.

Although his acting earned him praise from the critics, Downey had never starred in a blockbuster. None of his films had done very well at the box office. Given his reputation, and the fact that he'd never had a hit movie, studios weren't exactly lining up to hire him.

Yet Downey wanted the role—badly. He was already over 40, and he knew that his chance to star in a big-budget superhero movie was about to pass him by forever. Few studios were clamoring for a middle-aged superhero. Yet, Downey knew he could play this character.

Favreau saw the possibility in him. Like Downey, the character Tony Stark had fallen pretty low in life and wanted to redeem himself. Stark was a complex guy, and Downey's acting had depth that went beyond the average superhero actor. "Downey wasn't the most obvious choice, but he understood what makes the character tick," Favreau explained.[2]

Favreau was sold. He had a harder time convincing studio executives, though. They didn't want to entrust an unpredictable actor with a huge movie franchise.

> **"There's people throughout time who have been notorious, and I get to be one of them."[3]**
>
> —ROBERT DOWNEY JR., INSIDE THE ACTOR'S STUDIO, 2006

Downey and Favreau working together on the set of *Iron Man*

Apologetically, Favreau told Downey he couldn't get the studio to give him the green light. Downey replied, "If you don't mind, I'm just going to keep imagining this is possible."[4]

Downey agreed to do a screen test, which is usually where young, inexperienced actors prove themselves. He studied, practiced, and worked harder than he'd worked to land any other film role except Charlie Chaplin. Favreau knew his instincts had been right. With the proof of Downey's ability to play Stark on film, he was finally able to convince the studio heads.

A BIG RISK PAYS OFF

Just as he had with other roles, Downey put everything he had into bringing Tony Stark to life. His efforts paid off. *Iron Man* earned more than $100 million in its opening weekend. It went on to gross more than $318 million in the United States alone.

No one who was involved with the film regretted their decision to hire Downey. Marvel Studios Chairman David Maisel was so pleased with Downey's box office draw that he bought him a Bentley—one of the world's most expensive cars. As one critic later explained it, "Downey was somehow born to play Iron Man/Stark, and his performance is easy, confident, [and] assured."[5]

Downey had survived a broken home, a divorce, drug abuse, and jail time. Many critics had predicted that he—and his career—would

IRON MAN SUIT

The original costume made for *Iron Man*, called the Mark I, weighed 90 pounds (40 kg). It was so heavy that a stuntman fell over while wearing it. To prevent the same thing from happening to Downey, a digital version of the suit was also created.

Downey and his wife Susan walked the red carpet at the German premiere of *Iron Man* on April 22, 2008.

never survive. As fans lined up to see *Iron Man* and screamed Downey's name, he knew he'd not only survived. He'd secured his place as one of the great leading men in movie history.

||||||||||||

Robert Downey Jr. lived in Greenwich Village on Manhattan Island in New York City when he was young.

CHAPTER 2
An Unconventional Childhood

||||||||||||||||||||||||||||||||||||||||||||||||||||

Robert Downey Jr.'s childhood was quite unlike the upbringing of most US kids in the 1970s. His father didn't carry a briefcase to an office job each day. His mother wasn't a stay-at-home housewife.

Robert grew up in an unconventional home. His father, Robert Downey Sr., was an alternative filmmaker whose movies deal with unusual and often bizarre subjects.

The star of many of these avant-garde films was Robert's mother, actress and singer Elsie Ford. In 1963, Ford and Downey Sr. welcomed their first child, Allyson. Two years later, on April 4, 1965, Robert John Downey Jr. was born in New York City. He was named after his father only because his parents still hadn't come up with a name for him in the cab on their way to the hospital for the birth. Years later, when his son's fame had eclipsed his own, Downey Sr. said he regretted his decision to share his name with his child. "Look, whatever you do, don't name your kid after yourself," he warned others. "He might turn out to be more well known than you and it'll be very traumatizing."[1]

||||||||||||||||||||||||||||||||||||||||||||||||||||||||

PUTNEY SWOPE ||||||||||||||||||||||||||||||||||||||||||||||||||||||||||||||||||

Downey Sr.'s most famous movie was *Putney Swope*, which was released in 1969. In the satirical film, an African-American man is put in charge of an all-white advertising agency. He renames the firm *Truth & Soul* and proceeds to release a series of brutally honest—and wildly successful—ads. The film was an underground classic, but it never became a hit with mainstream audiences.

LOOSE PARENTING

Robert and Allyson spent their early years in Greenwich Village, a neighborhood in New York City. Creative people were always hanging around their apartment—actors and filmmakers. The family even had an occasional visit from political activists, including Abbie Hoffman, a protest organizer of the 1960s.

Robert was barely in kindergarten when his father cast him in his movie, *Pound*. "I'm almost certain it was because it was a lot less trouble than dealing with child labor," he said years later.[2]

The 1970 film tells the story of a group of dogs waiting to be adopted from a New York City kennel. It isn't an animated movie, and human actors played each of the dogs. Five-year-old Robert played a puppy.

As a child, Robert was treated like a little adult. He was allowed to sit in on his father's poker games. He watched—and later participated—as his father smoked marijuana with friends. At just 13, Robert was allowed to travel to Vermont by himself to visit his sister at school.

The lack of structure and routine had its ups and downs. By the mid-1970s, Downey Sr. struggled with drugs and his career. The Downey family went through periods in which they had plenty of money, followed by times when the electricity and phone were cut off.

Downey Sr. often uprooted his wife and children to work on a movie. After the release of *Putney Swope*, the Downeys packed up and headed for London, England. Robert found the teachers in London were very strict. He spent a good part of his school days standing in the corner of his classroom as punishment for disobeying.

||||||||||||||||||||||||||||||||||||||||||||||||||||||||||||

DIVORCE—AND YET ANOTHER MOVE

Downey Sr.'s drug use and shaky career were taking their toll on his relationship with his wife. In the late 1970s, he and Elsie divorced. Allyson went to live with Downey Sr. in Los Angeles, California. Robert moved to New York with his mother. Their apartment was cramped and dark, with protective bars on the windows. He spent most of his time hanging out with his friends in Greenwich Village's Washington Square Park.

When he was fifteen and the tiny apartment became too confining, Robert left his mother in New York and moved to Los Angeles with his father. It wasn't just more space he was craving. Watching his parents make movies had led to a fascination with film, and Robert knew he wanted to become an actor.

||||||||||||||||||||||||||||||||||||||||||||||||||||

SANTA MONICA HIGH

In Los Angeles, Robert first attended Lincoln Junior High School. Then he switched to Santa Monica High School. Actor Martin Sheen's kids also went to Santa Monica High. Robert spent a lot of time

CAR TROUBLE |||||||||||||||||||||||||||||||||||||||||||||||||||||||||||

As a teen, Robert had a habit of getting into trouble. While at a party one night, friend Chris Bell left Robert alone for a few minutes in his mother's Mercedes. The next thing Bell knew, Robert was in Santa Monica Police custody. He had driven off in the car drunk, gotten lost, and asked—of all people—a policeman for directions. It would be the first of several DUI (driving under the influence) charges Robert would face.

with his middle son, Ramon. When Robert was cast as Will Parker in the school play *Oklahoma!*, it was Ramon who taught him how to tap dance.

With only a handful of tiny roles in his father's movies under his belt, Robert had his sights set on celebrity. Classmates remember him bragging about someday becoming a movie star. Already he had a superstar-sized ego.

Years spent traveling the world and hanging out with actors, activists, and writers had also given Robert a worldly and mysterious quality. "There was a little bit of a mystique about him," said high school friend Chris Bell.[3]

Robert was into acting, his friends, and girls. School, however, didn't hold much interest for him. He'd show up in the morning, then scale the 20-foot- (6-m-) high chain-link fence that surrounded the school's perimeter to escape for a few hours. He only returned to school for theater class.

One day, in his junior year, Robert's guidance counselor called him into her office. Robert was a smart kid, but he'd been having trouble keeping up his grades. She told him he'd have to attend

Robert's high school yearbook photograph from junior year,
the same year he dropped out of high school

summer school. He refused. When the counselor
called Downey Sr., he sided with his son, saying,
"Sure, whatever he wants to do, as long as he gets
a job and is productive." Robert told the guidance
counselor, "I told you so."[4] He walked out of her
office—and his school—never to return again.

It would be years of waiting tables and taking tiny roles before Downey landed a spot in a major movie, appearing in *Tuff Turf* in 1985.

CHAPTER 3

Making It as an Actor

‖‖

After quitting high school, Downey had one goal—to become a famous actor. When Downey first told his father that he wanted to act, the reaction wasn't what he had expected. "I think he was indifferent," he said. "My dad says anybody can act and few can direct and nobody can write. On a scale of one to ten, being an actor was about the least honorable of those three."[1]

Downey might not have landed big roles in his early days of acting, but his lack of success didn't deflate his ego. He went to great lengths to get his name known, even if it meant offending every producer and director he met. Allyson recalls her brother pulling stunts such as going to an audition for a movie with an all African-American cast, then convincing every actor in the waiting room that he'd landed the part. When a producer once asked him, "How do you support yourself when you're not working as an actor?" Downy replied, "My spine."[3] He didn't get the part.

His father's words paint a different picture. Apparently, Downey Sr. thought his son had real talent. "When we put him in *Pound*, he resisted, but by the time he left you could see that's exactly what he wanted. He was very good from the beginning," he said.[2]

||||||||||||||||||||||||||||||||||||||||||||||||||||||

WAITING FOR A BREAK

At age 17, Downey moved back to New York to pursue his dream of becoming an actor. Fame and fortune would have to wait, though. While Downey auditioned, he bussed tables at Central Falls, a restaurant in the New York neighborhood

Soho. Working as a busboy didn't earn Downey enough money to afford a place of his own. He had to share his sister's small apartment on West Eighty-Fourth Street.

To make life even more challenging, Downey Sr. cut off his son financially at age 18. Downey's father warned him not to call for money, even if he was starving. Downey didn't have his father's blessing—or his help. He also didn't have much formal acting training. He'd learned the craft of acting by carefully watching friends who were in the business and by working hard.

Finally, Downey landed a few bit parts in local theater and off-Broadway productions, including "Alms for the Middle Class" and the musical "American Passion." An agent saw one of the shows, liked the young actor, and took him on as a client. Downey was on his way.

|||||||||||||||||||||||||||||||||||||||||||||||||||||||||||

MAYBE IT'S YOU

In 1983, Downey finally landed a part in a movie that wasn't his father's. *Baby It's You* is director

John Sayles's film about two New Jersey teenagers (played by Rosanna Arquette and Vincent Spano) who fall in love. Downey worked on the film for weeks, only to have his part cut down to just one scene. He had so little screen time his friends teasingly called the movie *Maybe It's You*.

A year later, Downey got another chance on screen when Director Michael Apted cast him in his movie *Firstborn*. The film starred acting veterans Terri Garr and Peter Weller, as well as young actress Sarah Jessica Parker. Though she was just 19, the same age as Downey, Parker had already landed several big projects, including a lead role in the television series *Square Pegs* and a part in the movie *Footloose*. She'd also played Annie on Broadway.

Parker couldn't help but notice Downey, with his spiked hair and glasses covered in Superman stickers. He stuck out, even among the better-known actors. Within two weeks of meeting, they had fallen in love and moved in together.

||||||||||||||||||||||||||||||||||||||||||||||||||||||||||

Downey, *wearing sunglasses*, and Parker fell in love
on the set of *Firstborn*.

BRAT PACK—AND BEYOND

In the early 1980s, one group of young actors
attracted a lot of media attention. Named "the
Brat Pack" by a 1985 *New York* magazine article,
they were the 1980s version of the 1950s Rat
Pack (which had featured Sammy Davis Jr., Frank
Sinatra, Peter Lawford, and Dean Martin). The
Brat Pack included Molly Ringwald, Rob Lowe,
Judd Nelson, Andrew McCarthy, James Spader,

Once they started making a lot of money from movies, Downey and Parker bought a house together in the Hollywood Hills. The house had once been owned by legendary comedic actor Charlie Chaplin.

The couple was young and free-spirited, and neighbors would often find themselves drenched by water balloons Downey and Parker hurled from their windows. They played at domesticity, living with two Persian cats—Mr. Smith and Scout—and joking about getting married in a Jewish ceremony with Spanish flamenco dancers. Parker even wore a diamond ring. Yet the two never married.

and Anthony Michael Hall. They starred in several popular films, including director John Hughes's *Sixteen Candles* and *The Breakfast Club*.

A few young actors at the time crossed paths with the Brat Pack without actually becoming part of the group. Downey was one of them. He starred in a couple of Brat Pack-era movies, including *Tuff Turf* with Spader and *Weird Science* with Hall, both of which were released in 1985.

Though his stint with the Brat Pack was temporary, a lifelong friendship grew out of it. On the Universal Studios set of *Weird Science*,

Downey and Hall hit it off right away. It was Hall who convinced Hughes to cast Downey in *Weird Science*. "He was just the most generous, helpful, and truly one of the great hilarious talents that I had the fortune of working with," Downey said of his friend.[4]

After a couple of Brat Pack movies, Downey moved on. He starred in a 1985 television miniseries about Italian dictator Benito Mussolini, in which he got to play opposite Academy Award–winning actor George C. Scott. Then his career switched gears again.

||||||||||||||||||||||||||||||||||||||||||||||||||||||||

SATURDAY NIGHT LIVE

In 1985, *Saturday Night Live*, NBC's late-night comedy skit show, was in a slump. The show's creator, Lorne Michaels, hired several exciting young comedians in an attempt to revive the show's sagging ratings. One of those comedians was 17-year-old Anthony Michael Hall.

Hall convinced Michaels to also audition Downey. At the audition, Downey performed a skit in which he imitated a drunken man he'd seen at a Beverly Hills nightclub. His improvisation was funny enough to land him the job.

Downey did celebrity impressions and created a few characters, none of which were very memorable. By the following season, Downey was off the show.

||||||||||||||||||||||||||||||||||||||||||||||||||||||||||||

LEADING MAN AT LAST

In the late 1980s, director James Toback was looking for a charismatic young actor to play Ringwald's love interest in *The Pick-Up Artist*. The character Jack Jericho reflected the movie's title—he spent most of his days engaged in the art of picking up women, or convincing them to date him. During his audition, Downey was his usual witty and charming self. Within a minute of meeting him, Toback knew he had found Jack Jericho. Unfortunately, *The Pick-Up Artist* was a box office flop in 1987, but as its lead Downey finally earned the attention of film critics. Pauline Kael of the *New Yorker* wrote, "Downey, whose soul is floppy eared, gives the movie a fairy-tale sunniness."[5]

With his lead role in *The Pick-Up Artist*,
Downey's career finally began to take off.

The Pick-Up Artist also caught the attention of
other Hollywood directors. It led that same year to
a lead role in *Less Than Zero*—a movie that secured
Downey's reputation for more than just his acting.

||||||||||

During the late 1980s, Parker grew increasingly worried about Downey's drug use.

CHAPTER 4

Deep into Drugs

||||||||||||||||||||||||||||||||||||||||||||||||||||||||||||||||||||||||||||||||||||||||||||||||||||||||

Downey had grown up around drugs. When he was a child, it was perfectly normal for him to watch his dad's friends smoke marijuana joints. During one of his dad's parties, when Downey was just eight years old, his father thought it would be funny to pass the joint to him. Downey took a puff. "And suddenly I knew I had made a terrible, stupid mistake," Downey Sr. recalled.[1] Looking back, Downey didn't blame his father for getting him hooked on drugs. "It was such a permissive time. And it was that culture," he said.[2]

By his teens, Downey was already well established in the New York party scene. Within a few years, drugs had become a dangerous habit he couldn't shake.

Live-in girlfriend Sarah Jessica Parker saw Downey's drug use getting more and more serious. Still, she thought she could change her boyfriend. "I did not recognize the signs," she said. "I was innocent in so many ways. I thought, 'Well, I will help him.' I didn't think that addiction was something that would impose itself on us. I was very wrong."[3]

|||||||||||||||||||||||||||||||||||||||||||||||||||||||||||||||

GIRLFRIEND BECOMES MOTHER |||||||||||||||||||||||||||||||||||||||||||||

By the mid-1980s, Parker and Downey were living together like husband and wife. Yet their relationship was becoming more and more like mother and child. Parker helped Downey open a bank account and hired an accountant to manage his new money. Every morning, she made sure he got out of bed and went to work. "If he did not, I was there to cover for him, find him, clean him up, and get him to the set or theater," she said.[4]

Downey's drug use in the 1987 film *Less Than Zero* mirrored his drug use in real life.

LESS THAN ZERO

Despite his increasing drug use, Downey was still able to work. In fact, his star as an actor just kept rising. After *The Pick-Up Artist*, he got a lot of interest from Hollywood directors. He was brought in to audition for *Less Than Zero*, a movie about three rich friends who reconnect after high school.

Downey wowed director Marek Kanievska immediately. Downey was given the role of Julian, a spoiled rich kid whose father wanted nothing to do with him. The character also struggled with a drug

In *Less Than Zero*, Downey's character Julian dies of a drug overdose. During the making of the film, Downey was spiraling into addiction, and his fellow actors feared he'd share the same fate. "You had the feeling, is this guy going to make it? Is what happens to Julian going to happen to Robert?" his costar Jamie Gertz said.[6]

Loree Rodkin, Downey's manager at the time, was also worried about her client. "When I went to the screening of *Less Than Zero*, I burst into tears, [because] it was such a foreshadowing, but Robert laughed and said, 'Don't be stupid. This isn't how it will end up.'"[7]

addiction. In many ways, playing Julian was like reenacting an exaggeration of his own life.

As Julian, Downey gave a performance so realistic that critic Roger Ebert called it "scary."[5] In the movie Julian's drug addiction cost him his life. Many of Downey's friends worried—would the same thing happen to him?

||||||||||||||||||||||||||||||||||||||||||||||||||||

REHAB—TAKE 1

In the late 1980s, Downey was still lucid enough to realize he was in trouble. Drugs were eroding his ability to function. "You start to realize you're not dealing with your life," he said. "You're living it, but you're not dealing with anything."[8]

In 1987, Downey checked himself into Sierra Tucson, a 325-acre (132-ha) rehabilitation facility in the Santa Catalina Mountains of Arizona. Downey cycled in and out of rehab over the next decade. He'd stop using drugs for a while, only to pick them up again soon afterwards. Soon Downey was using many drugs, including cocaine, pot, heroin, and crack.

|||||||||||

Downey played a football player in *Johnny Be Good*, one movie in a string of 1980s flops.

Bad Choices

||||||||||||||||||||||||||||||||||||||||||||||||||||||||||||||||||||||||||||||

As Downey's drug use grew more and more out of control, he started taking roles in worse movies. In the late 1980s, he did several forgettable movies in a row, including *Johnny Be Good* with friend Anthony Michael Hall and his father's comedy *Rented Lips*.

In *Johnny Be Good*, Downey played the teammate of Hall's character, Johnny Walker—a high school football star. Many critics considered the film nap-worthy, but a few thought Downey rose above the drab script. The *New York Times* reviewer wrote, "Mr. Downey seems to belong in another, better movie . . ."[1]

While *Johnny Be Good* was forgettable, *Rented Lips* was pretty much forgotten. Downey's character, Wolf Dangler, spends much of the movie dressed in a Nazi jacket with no pants and high black boots. The role allowed him to act as crazy and free as he wanted. The only trouble was, very few people wanted to see the end result.

In 1989, Downey appeared in three more unsuccessful movies—*1969*, *True Believer*, and *Chances Are*. The movie *1969* tells the story of two college students who object to the Vietnam War. Downey starred opposite Kiefer Sutherland and Winona Ryder. The film earned less than $6 million in the United States.

In *True Believer*, Downey played an idealistic young attorney named Roger Baron who takes on the case of a Korean man unjustly charged with murder. In the movie, Downey teamed up with Oscar-nominated actor James Woods. Woods liked him right away. He nicknamed Downey "Binky"

James Woods, *right*, was impressed with Downey's acting in *True Believer*.

and joked about adopting him. "I think [Downey] is the finest of the young actors," Woods said. "He really has that magic gift—he's a real natural."[2]

Next came *Chances Are*, in which Downey starred as the reincarnation of Cybill Shepherd's dead husband. Shepherd was famous for starring in the 1980s television sitcom *Moonlighting*. From Shepherd, Downey learned how to take his time with his lines. Though his acting might have benefited from the movie, his reputation didn't. *Chances Are* was another flop.

AIR GENERICA

By the end of the 1980s, Downey had made a string of mediocre movies. Meanwhile, he was turning down really good roles—such as *The Freshman* starring screen legend Marlon Brando. Matthew Broderick ended up taking the part.

Instead, in 1990 Downey signed on to do *Air America*. In the movie, he played a young pilot who flies food, medical supplies, and weapons to anticommunist fighters in Laos during the Vietnam War. He took the role because he wanted to act alongside Mel Gibson. Downey also wanted to star in a big-budget action movie. The film definitely was a big-budget operation. *Air America* cost $35 million to produce. It was shot in London, Los Angeles, and Thailand. Five hundred crewmembers worked on the film. Yet despite its massive budget, *Air America* didn't break even, earning just $31 million at the box office.

After *Air America* (which he later called Air Generica), Downey swore off action movies. He started looking for more meaningful parts. Downey explained,

Although he enjoyed working with Mel Gibson in *Air America*, Downey avoided roles in action movies for years after.

You feel you have to do the commercial films in order to keep your visibility high and your agents and managers happy, but you want to do films that are important, too.[3]

A BREAKUP . . .
AND A WEDDING

By the early 1990s, Downey's father was remarried to writer Laura Ernst. The couple lived just blocks away from Downey in Los Angeles, which gave

While Downey experimented with his acting style, he also tried his hand at other artistic endeavors, such as poetry, painting, and writing. Wearing a black turtleneck, he'd perform his poems at Los Angeles clubs. One of his poems was a takeoff on Edgar Allen Poe's "The Tell-Tale Heart." In it, he wrote, "He chopped up the body like a gourmet magnifico . . . And put those pieces under the floorboard very specifico."[5]

father and son a chance to reconnect. Downey also acted in another one of his father's movies, *Too Much Sun*, which Ernst cowrote.

Downey Sr. was thrilled that his son had settled down with Parker. He thought Parker was good for taming Downey's wild ways. "I thank God for Sarah Jessica Parker," he told *People* magazine in the mid-1980s. "Without her, Robert would go at 100 miles an hour [160 km/h] into a brick wall."[4]

However, Parker and Downey's domestic bliss didn't last. In 1991, after seven years together, Downey and Parker broke up. Their differences ultimately ended their relationship. Parker liked quiet evenings at home, and she had grown increasingly frustrated at Downey's escalating drug use. She'd made attempt after attempt to help him, but he wouldn't stop using.

When they broke up, Downey told reporters how much he worshipped Parker—and how much she'd done for him. "She was there for me every step of the way. I think she saved my life. No, I know she saved my life," he said.[6]

Parker called Downey "one of those tortured souls."[7] She said she constantly worried she would get a call one day saying Downey had been found dead of a drug overdose. Eventually, Parker was able to move on with her life. In 1997, she married actor Matthew Broderick.

It didn't take Downey long to move on. On May 29, 1992, just months after Parker left him, he married actress and singer Deborah Falconer. The two had met at an art gallery while Downey was out on a date with another woman. They hit it off right away. Falconer and Downey were married at a private ceremony in Walnut Creek, California.

Falconer moved into the same Hollywood house Downey had shared with Parker. Before Falconer arrived, Downey wanted to clear out the energy from his relationship with Parker. He hired

Downey attended the movie premiere for *Hearts and Souls* with pregnant wife Deborah Falconer in August 1993.

a woman to perform a blessing ritual, singing throughout the house to disperse the spirits of girlfriends past.

||||||||||||||||||||||||||||||||||||||||||||||||||||||

BECOMING A FATHER

On September 7, 1993, Falconer gave birth to a son, whom the couple named Indio. The name is Spanish for "Indian." Downey chose Hall to be the baby's godfather. Once he became a father, Downey realized he had to end his on-again, off-again drug habit. He had to stay sober for his son.

> "Our marriage and having a child probably kept me from going off the rails completely, but it wasn't enough to right the ship."[8]
>
> —ROBERT DOWNEY JR.

The family moved into a two-story home in Malibu, a city just north of Los Angeles. For a while, the marriage went smoothly. But by the mid-1990s, Downey was heavily using drugs again. In April 1996, Falconer took Indio and moved out of the house.

||||||||||||

Downey appeared with actress Marisa Tomei in *Chaplin*.

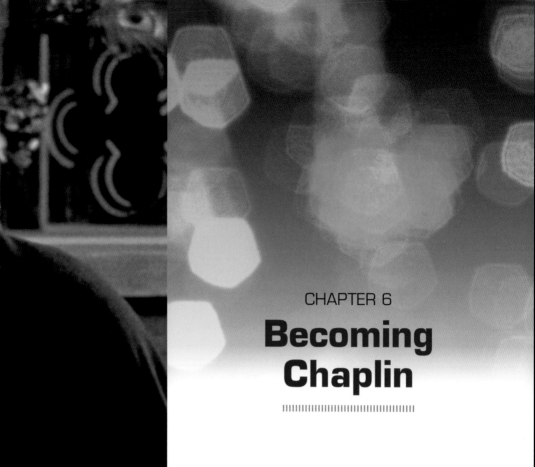

CHAPTER 6

Becoming Chaplin

IIIIIIIIIIIIIIIIIIIIIIIIIIIIIIIIIIIIIIIIIIII

After a string of bad movies, Downey's acting career was looking bleak. He needed a hit—one that would cement his talent and credibility as an actor. Downey thought director Sir Richard Attenborough might have just that movie.

In 1982, Attenborough had made a film about Mohandas Gandhi, the man who led India to its independence from British rule. The movie transformed actor Ben Kingsley into Gandhi. It was hailed as an instant classic and earned eight Oscars, including a best director award for Attenborough. A decade later, Attenborough was looking for an actor to transform into another legendary historical figure—British film star Charlie Chaplin.

Not just any actor could play Chaplin. The diminutive British actor was considered one of the most brilliant comedians in screen history. Whoever played him had to have just the right attributes. First, he needed to be short enough. Chaplin stood only approximately 5 feet 5 inches (1.6 m) tall. He also needed to be able to mimic the many different British accents Chaplin had adopted during his lifetime. This actor needed the agility to pull off Chaplin's distinctive walk and physical comedy. And he needed the range to play Chaplin from his teens into his eighties.

BIG NAMES CONSIDERED FOR CHAPLIN

Downey beat out 30 other actors for the role of Charlie Chaplin. Among those considered for the part were some of Hollywood's leading men, including Dustin Hoffman, Billy Crystal, and Robin Williams.

SHARING CHAPLIN'S HOUSE |||||||||||||||||||||||||||||||||||||||||||

Years before playing Chaplin on film, Downey slept in the British actor's bedroom. Downey lived in the same Spanish-style house in the Hollywood Hills that had been built for Chaplin in the 1920s. In 2011, the three-bedroom house—and its cinematic history—went on sale for $1.725 million.

Downey was convinced he was that actor. He'd always been a big Chaplin fan. He was just 5 feet 8 inches (1.7 m) tall. He'd even lived in the same Hollywood home that had been built for Chaplin in 1926.

When Downey arrived for his meeting with Attenborough wearing black boots and spiked hair, the director didn't see a hint of Charlie Chaplin. Downey assured Attenborough that he was the one actor who could pull off Chaplin. He said, "One day you'll come back to me."[1] Then he left.

Attenborough finally agreed to let Downey do a screen test. To prepare, Downey spent hours rehearsing Chaplin's voice and mannerisms. He read Chaplin's biography and watched his movies over and over again. During the screen test, Downey responded to the director's questions

Downey, on the set of *Chaplin* with director Richard Attenborough, worked hard to bring Chaplin to life.

as Chaplin. In detail, he described the film he was currently shooting and the parties he was attending. His impersonation of the British actor was dead-on. Downey not only conveyed Chaplin's speech and movement—he captured all of the turmoil and drive that had made Chaplin a genius. And he got the part.

||||||||||||||||||||||||||||||||||||||||||||||||||||||||||||

BECOMING CHARLIE CHAPLIN

Downey put even more effort into bringing Chaplin to life on screen. He worked with a movement coach to precisely mimic Chaplin's posture and walk. A dialect coach helped him capture Chaplin's voice and accents exactly. Other coaches helped him learn to play the violin and hit a tennis ball left-handed like Chaplin.

Downey was obsessed with accurately portraying Chaplin. He'd call Attenborough in the middle of the night to go over the tiniest detail of Chaplin's life. His intensity might have been a little over the top, but the result was worth the effort. Geraldine Chaplin (who played her own

STEPPING INTO CHAPLIN'S SHOES

While preparing to play Chaplin, Downey didn't just study his lines. He completely absorbed himself in Chaplin's life. Downey watched Chaplin's movies over and over. He read biographies of the silent film actor from cover to cover. He even walked a few steps in Chaplin's shoes.

At the Museum of the Moving Image in London, Downey tried on Chaplin's shoes. They fit—perfectly. He also tried on the suit Chaplin wore in the 1936 film *Modern Times*. In its pocket he discovered a cigar—a prop that may have come straight from a scene in the film.

grandmother in the movie) told reporters how eerily similar Downey had become to her father.

Although critics gave the movie a tepid response, they loved Downey. Vincent Canby of the *New York Times* called Downey, "Close to brilliant when he does some of Charlie's early vaudeville and film sketches."[2] Downey was nominated for a Best Actor Oscar, though he lost out to Al Pacino for *Scent of a Woman*. Still, *Chaplin* had transformed Downey into a real movie star.

1990s MOVIE ROLES

Downey followed up *Chaplin* with a few smaller films in the early 1990s. There was *Heart and Souls* in 1993, a comedy in which he played a man haunted by four different spirits. Then he had a small part in *Short Cuts*. And in 1994, he played a sleazy Australian tabloid television host in *Natural Born Killers*.

As an Oscar nominee for *Chaplin*, Downey began demanding a seven-figure paycheck. He earned $2.25 million for just seven weeks of work on *Only You*. The movie starred Marisa Tomei as a woman who travels to Italy in search of the man she believes she is destined to marry. Downey played the charming leading man. Although the film was just a light romance, Downey and Tomei's on-screen chemistry sold critics on the film.

SLIPPING AGAIN

As sunny as he was on screen, Downey's dark side hadn't deserted him. He had been using drugs consistently while filming his movies. He was even taking drugs while shooting *Chaplin*, but he managed to turn in such a good performance that director Attenborough didn't criticize him for it.

By the mid-1990s, Downey's drug use was again getting out of control—and so was his behavior. In 1995, he filmed the period movie *Restoration*. Downey starred as physician Robert Merivel, who worked for England's King Charles II in the seventeenth century. He perfected Merivel's English accent and even learned to play the Baroque oboe. But his behavior on the movie set earned him negative headlines. Downey was notoriously nasty to costar Hugh Grant. Then Downey showed up for the film's screening at an elegant hotel in Germany wearing a T-shirt, screaming "Everybody dance now!"[3]

That same year, Downey starred in the ensemble film *Home for the Holidays*, which is about a crazy family Thanksgiving. He was smoking heroin throughout the filming. For the first time, he was not only getting high at night after shooting had finished. Now he was coming to work that way too. Director Jodie Foster expressed her concerns in a note to Downey that read:

Off camera, Downey and his *Restoration* costar Hugh Grant, *left,* did not get along.

Listen, I'm not worried about you on this film. You're not losing it or nodding out and you're giving a great performance. I'm worried about your thinking you can get away with doing this on another film.[4]

By the time he starred in his father's 1997 movie *Hugo Pool*, Downey was in bad shape. He looked thin, pale, and sickly. He delivered his lines in bursts of manic energy. One critic called his

Downey followed up his success in *Chaplin* with a string of failed movies. None of the other films he made in the early 1990s did well at the box office. Downey started believing he was box-office poison. "If you want your film to have a lousy opening weekend just throw me in it, 'cause I've never been in a film that was a big hit," he said.[6]

performance "beyond bad" and gave the movie an F grade.[5]

That same year, director Mike Figgis was casting the part of a choreographer dying of AIDS for his movie *One Night Stand*. Downey certainly looked the part. When he showed up for his meeting with Figgis at a Beverly Hills restaurant, he was two hours late and barefoot. He appeared sick and gaunt, weighing only approximately 140 pounds (64 kg). Downey looked like a man on the edge. No one knew just how far he would fall.

||||||||||

Downey's drug use made him lose weight, making his portrayal of a person suffering from AIDS in the film *One Night Stand* more realistic.

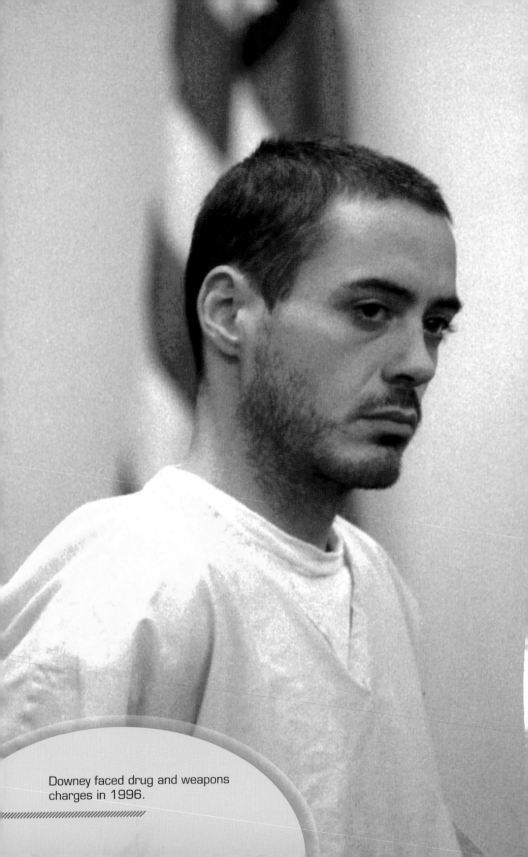

Downey faced drug and weapons charges in 1996.

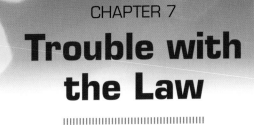

CHAPTER 7

Trouble with the Law

|||||||||||||||||||||||||||||||||||||||||||||

The year 1996 would prove to be a long, strange one for Downey. On June 23, Los Angeles police clocked Downey's Ford Explorer on the Pacific Coast Highway going more than 70 miles per hour (110 km/h) where the speed limit was only 50 miles per hour (80 km/h).

The officer who pulled him over noticed that Downey was acting strangely. A search of his car revealed a stash of illegal items—cocaine, heroin, and an unloaded .357 magnum handgun. When Downey later appeared in court, Malibu Municipal Judge Lawrence J. Mira convicted him on charges of felony drug possession, driving under the influence, and possessing a concealed weapon. The judge gave him three years probation. During that time, Downey would have to submit to random drug tests and receive counseling for his drug use.

|||||||||||||||||||||||||||||||||||||||||||||||||||||||||||||

THE "GOLDILOCKS" INCIDENT

On the evening of July 16, 1996, Lisa Curtis walked into her 11-year-old son, Daniel's, bedroom in their Malibu home. A lump lay in the bed. When she pulled back the covers, she got quite a shock. Lying there was a strange man, fast asleep. It was Downey. Curtis called 911. In the tape of the call, Downey can be heard snoring in the background. The police took him away.

Curtis and her family were Downey's neighbors, living on the same Malibu street. At first, Downey made the excuse that his limo driver had dropped

Lisa Curtis explained to reporters how she found Downey asleep in her son's bed.

him off at the wrong house. But, the heroin police found in his blood sample told a different story.

The event became known as the "Goldilocks" incident, after the storybook character who wandered into the Three Bears' house and fell asleep in Baby Bear's bed.

Judge Mira sent Downey to a drug rehab program at the Exodus Recovery Center in Marina

Del Ray, California. Just two days after he arrived, Downey escaped out a window. When he arrived at a friend's house, police quickly recaptured him. This time, Judge Mira set bail at $250,000 and booked Downey into a cell at the Los Angeles County Jail.

In court again on July 22, Downey appeared pale in contrast to his bright orange jumpsuit. Judge Mira ordered him into a six-month supervised drug recovery program.

||||||||||||||||||||||||||||||||||||||||||||||||||||||||||||||||||

FALLING OFF THE WAGON

For a while, it seemed as though Downey was trying to get clean. Then in September 1997, he started using drugs again. Once again, Downey was brought in front of Judge Mira.

Downey tearfully described how he'd been hooked on drugs since age eight. The judge wasn't moved. On December 8, he sentenced Downey to 180 days in the Los Angeles County Jail.

Downey wasn't given any special treatment in jail. In February 1998, two prisoners attacked Downey, punching and kicking him. In March,

After the disastrous *Air America* in 1990, Downey swore he'd never make another action movie. But by 1998 he was deep into drugs and over his head in financial trouble. So when he was offered *U.S. Marshals*, the sequel to the 1993 Harrison Ford movie *The Fugitive*, he took it. Downey called it, "Probably the worst action movie of all time."[1] He said, "I'd rather wake up in jail for a TB [tuberculosis] test than have to wake up another morning knowing I'm going to the set of *U.S. Marshals*."[2]

Downey was released after serving four months of his sentence. He was sent to a residential drug treatment center to serve out the rest of his time.

TWO GIRLS AND A GUY— A SECOND CHANCE ON SCREEN

In the late 1980s, director James Toback had helped launch Downey's career when he cast him in *The Pick-Up Artist*. A decade later, he decided to stage Downey's comeback. Toback wrote a script for Downey, *Two Girls and a Guy*. It is the story of two women who go to their boyfriend's apartment,

Downey appeared in *Two Girls and a Guy* with Natasha Gregson Wagner, *left*, and Heather Graham, *right*.

only to discover he is dating both of them at the same time.

Two Girls and a Guy was shot in just 11 days. The entire movie is set in one location—the boyfriend's apartment. The budget was only approximately $1 million, half of which went to pay Downey's salary. In the movie, Downey was as capable an actor as ever, but something had changed. "It was like watching a candle burning at both ends," one reporter noted. "There was the sense of watching someone gifted, but doomed."[3]

|||||||||||||||||||||||||||||||||||||||||||||||||||||||||||||||

THE LAST STRAW

By the late 1990s, it did seem as though Downey was doomed. He was totally broke, and he owed more than $1 million in unpaid taxes. On the surface, Downey looked like he was making an effort to recover. He told reporters he was clean and sober. He acted in a couple of movies—*Wonder Boys* with Michael Douglas and *Black and White* with Brooke Shields. But behind the scenes, he was missing his court-appointed drug tests. Downey was using again.

> **"It's like I've got a shotgun in my mouth and I've got a finger on the trigger and I like the taste of the gun metal."[4]**
>
> —*DOWNEY EXPLAINING HIS DRUG USE*

In 1999, Downey violated his parole again and found himself back in court. His lawyer, celebrity attorney Robert Shapiro, argued for another chance at rehabilitation instead of jail time. He called Downey's drug addiction "a disease he can't control."[5] Telling Downey he had no other choice, on February 11, Judge Mira issued his sentence: three years in jail.

||||||||||||||||||||||||||||||||||||||||||||||||||||||||||||

DOING HARD TIME

In August, Downey was sent to the California Substance Abuse Treatment Facility in Corcoran, a prison for people convicted of drug offenses. In prison he wasn't Robert Downey Jr., the actor. He was inmate number P50522.

Downey's "home" was Cell 17 in F-1 Block. He roomed with four other prisoners: Big Al, Timmons, Figueroa Slim (Charles Bell), and Sugar Bear. They called him "Mo Downey."

The man who had recently earned more than $2 million per movie now made eight cents an hour scrubbing dishes in the prison's kitchen. He woke up early every day and spent most of his days either working or in drug counseling.

"It's an unimaginably awful situation," Downey said of his time in prison.[6] He compared it to a

5'0

CSATF SP
P 5 0 5 2 2
D O W N E Y

Downey's mug shot showed his inmate number, P50522.

"death sentence."[7] One of the worst things about being there for Downey was that his son, Indio, knew he was in jail. Downey had wanted to tell Indio that he was on a spy mission to Yugoslavia, but Falconer insisted they tell their son the truth.

Despite Downey's misery, he realized that being in prison probably saved his life by pulling him off the self-destructive path he was on. Prison wasn't entirely awful. Downey used the downtime to express himself artistically and catch up on his academics. He wrote poems and painted watercolors. He earned his GED. And he read the many letters fans sent supporting him and wishing for his release.

Their wish was granted in August 2000 when Downey earned an early release from prison. He checked himself straight into Walden House, a drug treatment facility in Los Angeles. "It's nice to be able to walk outside and not have to wear a uniform anymore. Prison fashion is pretty limited,"

FANS STAY LOYAL

Downey's fans didn't abandon him when he went to prison. They not only stood by him during his incarceration, they even pushed for his release.

Devoted fans sent Downey hundreds of letters each week. He tried to respond to as many of those letters as possible. Fans also set up online petitions to get him released early from prison. At the April 2000 opening of *Black and White* in New York, people lined Union Square, holding up banners that read "Free Robert!" Not long afterward, Downey was freed from prison.

he joked of his new freedom.[8] He promised to work hard, stay healthy, and not slip back into his old habits. But for a drug addict, old habits can be hard to break.

||||||||||||||||||||||||||||||||||||||||||||||||||||||||||

ALLY MCBEAL

As Downey was leaving prison and settling into his new rehab facility, producer David E. Kelley was worried about the ratings of his television show *Ally McBeal*. He needed some new blood—a love interest for the title character. He thought Downey might be just the actor to breathe life back into the show.

At the time, Downey was a bad bet in Hollywood. No studio wanted to risk money on an actor who had just been released from prison. Kelley was willing to take the risk. "There's just something so uninhibited and so free and so uncensored about him," he raved.[9] He paid Downey $500,000 to play lawyer Larry Paul in eight episodes of *Ally McBeal*.

It was the first time Downey had starred in a television show, but he was an immediate hit. The

Downey's appearances in *Ally McBeal* opposite Calista Flockhart
helped rehabilitate his career.

show's ratings jumped 11 percent when he arrived.
Downey finished the eight episodes and signed on
to do two more. He showed up to work every day
on time and attended all of his counseling meetings
for his drug addiction. One television critic said
Downey's work on the show "may be as good as

anything anyone has done on a television series."[10] Downey's acting was so good, in fact, it earned him a Golden Globe award for Best Supporting Actor.

Soon Hollywood started calling again. Mel Gibson asked Downey to star in a stage production of Shakespeare's play *Hamlet*. Director Joe Roth called offering him a role in *America's Sweethearts* with Julia Roberts and Billy Crystal. Things were definitely looking up. After two months at the drug treatment center, Downey moved into a two-bedroom Hollywood apartment.

|||||||||||||||||||||||||||||||||||||||||||||||||||||||||||||

THE END OF THE ROAD

For the first time in many years, Downey's future looked bright. He was driving a ratings resurgence on a hit television show, and he was staying sober. Then he slipped.

On November 25, 2000, Palm Springs police received an anonymous phone call. The caller said there was a man with drugs in Room 311 of the Merv Griffin Resort Hotel. When police arrived at the upscale hotel, they found Downey. In his

In 2001, Downey was briefly allowed to leave his drug treatment center to work on an Elton John music video. The video was done in one shot as Downey walked through the empty rooms of a French mansion, lip-synching to the song "I Want Love." The honesty in his eyes revealed just how personal the lyrics were to him: "I want love, but it's impossible. A man like me, so irresponsible."[12]

room were more than 4 grams of cocaine and Valium pills.

Once again, Downey was arrested. During the arrest, one of the officers said to Downey, "Just because you are a movie star, that doesn't mean you can break the rules." Downey replied, "I'm not a movie star. I'm a guy with a drug problem."[11] He posted $15,000 bail and was released.

On April 24, 2001, while Downey was still out on bail, a police officer found him wandering around in an alley in Culver City, California. The officer didn't recognize Downey, but noticed that he was speaking too quickly and couldn't stand still. Downey was arrested yet again. This time he could have been sentenced to four years in prison.

Instead, he was sent back to a drug-treatment center for six months.

Downey's wife, Falconer, had finally had enough. She filed for divorce on January 23, 2001, taking custody of Indio. The divorce would not become final until April 2004, however. The Fox network fired Downey from *Ally McBeal*. He lost the role in *America's Sweethearts* to Hank Azaria. Downey was broke, out of work, and alone. Now that he'd hit absolute bottom, there was nowhere to go but up.

||||||||||||

As Downey gave up drug use, his role in the *Singing Detective* breathed new life into his career.

CHAPTER 8

Emerging from the Darkness

||||||||||||||||||||||||||||||||||||||||||||||||||||||||||||||||||||||||||||||||

The 1990s was a long, dark decade for Downey. He struggled with drug use and a series of arrests. In 2002, Downey's past drug charges were dismissed. His probation was finally over. He had finished his drug rehabilitation. Yet Downey still wasn't entirely free from his drug use.

Acting without the tethers of cocaine, heroin, and other drugs was liberating for Downey. "To act is to play an instrument, but how can you play the saxophone when it's filled with Crisco?" he told a journalist.[1] He said coffee and cigarettes were his last two addictions. He promised to eventually get rid of them, too.

One summer night in 2003, Downey went out for a drive. He'd been doing drugs for several days straight. Suddenly, the flashing lights he'd seen so many times before appeared in his rearview mirror. As the policeman pulled him over, Downey panicked. He thought of all the drugs that were hidden in his car. But the officer didn't search his car. He simply told Downey he needed to fix his license plate and sent him on his way.

A few days later, Downey was driving up the Pacific Coast Highway on his way to a friend's wedding when the seriousness of the situation fully hit him. If the officer had searched his car and found the drugs, he could have been sent back to rehab—or worse, back to jail. He realized he'd been given a second chance. Downey drove to the edge of the ocean and tossed every one of his drugs into the water.

As Downey was slowly pulling himself out of the darkness that had engulfed him for more than a decade, Mel Gibson called. He said he'd found the perfect role for Downey. Downey was reluctant to take the role, but he said yes. The movie Gibson had described was called *The Singing Detective*. Downey played crime writer Dan Dark, whose skin was disfigured by disease. Stuck in his hospital room, Dark imagined himself solving cases as the detective in his books.

SUPPORTING MEL GIBSON

Gibson and Downey had been friends since they made *Air America* together in 1990. Gibson had always supported Downey and his career. Gibson got him the role in *The Singing Detective* when most directors were reluctant to hire him. And when no insurance company would cover Downey's work on the film, Gibson stepped in and paid for the insurance himself.

So when Gibson got into trouble, getting arrested for a DUI in 2006 and later being accused of hurting his girlfriend, it was Downey's turn to stand up for his friend. "The truth is, he and I have a friendship that spans well over two decades and he's a stand-up guy; he always has been for me," Downey told Meredith Vieira on the *Today Show* in 2010.[2]

LOVE ON SET

In 2003, director Mathieu Kassovitz cast Downey in his thriller *Gothika* opposite actress Halle Berry. Downey played a therapist who helps Berry's character after she wakes up in an insane asylum with no memory of how she got there.

Filming *Gothika* was important to Downey's life for a very personal reason. On set, he met the woman of his dreams—the movie's producer, Susan Levin. Downey was still in the process of finalizing his divorce from Falconer at the time.

At first, Levin didn't share Downey's interest. She had no desire to date him. All she cared about was getting him to the set on time each day. In fact, she thought he was a little weird. Finally she

ON-SET ACCIDENT

To make a suspenseful thriller like *Gothika* often required the actors to get very physical. In one scene, Downey had to hold Berry down. As he restrained her arm, Berry resisted. Then suddenly Downey felt something snap. Berry's arm had broken. Although she had to wear a cast for several weeks, Berry didn't hold the incident against her costar. "It was a freak accident but we're good friends," she said.[3]

Acting requires a lot of memorization. Sometimes actors have to memorize pages and pages of dialogue. Every actor has his or her own technique for learning lines. Downey's technique is somewhat unusual.

First, he writes out all of his lines in one sloppy run-on sentence. Then he writes just the first letter of each word, creating one very long acronym. Finally, he reads the acronym as fast as he can, until he has it (and all of the lines buried within it) memorized.

agreed to go out on a dinner date with him. Soon, her feelings for Downey changed.

Downey proposed to Levin on November 6, 2003, one minute before the end of her thirtieth birthday. She agreed, but only on the condition that he stay sober. "I'm not doing that dance with you," she said. "I'm drawing a line in the sand here."[4] With Levin keeping him grounded, Downey promised to stay drug-free.

They were married on August 27, 2005, at an elegant estate in the Hamptons, a New York beachside resort. More than 100 guests attended, including actor Keanu Reeves and musicians Sting and Billy Joel. Instead of the traditional champagne

Downey and Levin married in 2005.

toast, the couple celebrated their nuptials by clinking glasses of nonalcoholic ginger spritzers.

At age 40, Downey was celebrating a kind of rebirth. He was off drugs, in love, and finally looking forward to the future. He and Levin bought a house in Malibu and settled into domestic life together. "It is almost like a perfectly normal life," he said. "Of course, I am afraid of falling back into the clutches of substance abuse—everybody is— but my wife is there for me."[5]

||||||||||||||||||||||||||||||||||||||||||||||||||||

NEW ROLES

Levin encouraged Downey to take bigger, more A-list roles with his newfound career focus. Still, Downey stayed low-key for the next couple of years. He took starring roles in smaller films, including the comedy/mystery *Kiss Kiss Bang Bang* with Val Kilmer and the animated sci-fi film *A Scanner Darkly* with Keanu Reeves and Winona Ryder. He also took smaller parts in big films, including Disney's *The Shaggy Dog* with Tim Allen and *Good Night and Good Luck*, directed by George Clooney.

IN HIS FATHER'S FOOTSTEPS

Downey's fellow actors looked at him with nothing but admiration. Jake Gyllenhaal, who costarred with him in the suspense thriller *Zodiac*, called working with Downey "a master class."[6] Seventeen-year-old actor Anton Yelchin learned a tremendous amount from studying Downey's work in *Charlie Bartlett*. "His range and his understanding of the freedom he has as an actor are so eye-opening," Yelchin said.[7] Finally, Downey had begun a career renaissance.

Downey voiced an animated character that looked just like him in *A Scanner Darkly*.

Downey illustrated the cover for his album *The Futurist*.

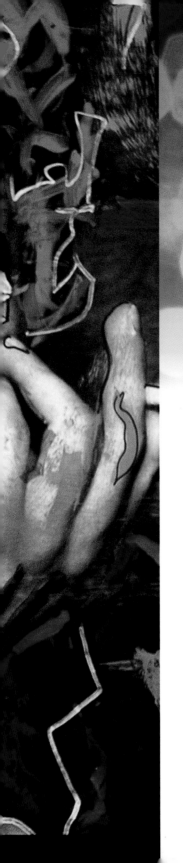

Recovery, Reinvention, and Career Rebirth

‖‖‖‖‖‖‖‖‖‖‖‖‖‖‖‖‖‖‖‖‖‖‖‖‖‖‖‖‖‖‖‖‖‖‖‖‖

Downey didn't just reinvent his life and acting career—he explored other facets of his creative talent as well. That exploration included the release of his first music album.

> "If this is a part of my story—and it is a story—when we are dealing with someone who has been around as long as I have and put themselves and their public at large through all these rollercoaster moments, then this is the part of the story when I have my comeback."[1]
>
> —ROBERT DOWNEY JR.

Music had always been a big part of Downey's life. He started singing and playing music around the same time he began acting. By age seven, Downey was playing the family piano without having had a single lesson. He taught himself how to play by mimicking a commercial jingle he'd heard on television.

Over the years, Downey had written and recorded a few songs. He penned the title track to his father's film *Too Much Sun*. He also composed songs for the sound tracks to *Two Girls and a Guy* and *Ally McBeal*. Now he wanted to create an album of his own original tracks. He recorded that album, *The Futurist*, with the help of composer and record producer Jonathan Elias. The CD was released in 2004.

Reviews of the album were mixed. While some critics praised his musical ability, others thought he should stick to acting. After calling *The Futurist* a "dribbly effort," *Entertainment Weekly*'s critic wrote, "And actors wonder why we tease them when they try to sing."[2] Downey wasn't worried by the criticism. "I figured if people don't like it, I could always use another dose of humility," he said.[3]

||||||||||||||||||||||||||||||||||||||||||||||||||||||||||||||||

ACTING SUCCESS

Though his music received mixed reviews, the response to his upcoming movie efforts was much more positive. In 2008, Downey staged what many critics believed to be his big movie comeback with *Iron Man*, a film that was both a critical and commercial success.

As self-made superhero Tony Stark, Downey led *Iron Man* to a $318 million windfall. *Time* magazine put Downey's starring role on its list of the ten top movie comebacks, writing, "Downey has entered the most potent part of his career . . ."[4]

By leading *Iron Man* to the top of the box office, Downey had proved he could carry a mega-blockbuster movie. He joined the list of Hollywood's most sought-after leading men. Almost immediately, Marvel Studios signed him on to do the sequel, *Iron Man 2*, which was released in 2010.

> "Right now, my BlackBerry is literally overloading and crashing and the phone is never not ringing. . . . It's crazy. Like a Super Bowl. Like a landslide. Like nothing I've ever experienced."[5]
>
> —ROBERT DOWNEY JR. ON THE ENTERTAINMENT INDUSTRY'S RESPONSE TO IRON MAN

Downey was also getting calls for other blockbuster films. Actor/director Ben Stiller offered Downey a role in his action/comedy *Tropic Thunder*. Downey was to play Kirk Lazarus, an Australian actor who becomes so obsessed with his role as black soldier Lincoln Osiris in a Vietnam War movie that he gets his skin dyed black. Filming began in 2007. Downey may have gotten at least some of the inspiration for the character from himself. His cast mates said he'd often talk to them as if he were Osiris. Downey played his character

Downey received critical acclaim for his role in *Tropic Thunder*.

so authentically that he was nominated for an Academy Award and a Golden Globe.

Downey followed up *Tropic Thunder* with *The Soloist*, a drama about a *Los Angeles Times* journalist who befriends a gifted but homeless musician, played by Jamie Foxx. The extras in the film were homeless people. After his own descent to rock bottom, Downey found the experience working with the homeless humbling.

Because he has been so successful in life, Downey believes it is important to contribute to charitable causes and help others. Based on his own life story, it is not surprising that one of his favorite causes is prison reform. In 2011, Downey met with then-governor of California Arnold Schwarzenegger and suggested reforms to help released prisoners integrate into normal society. Downey attends events and donates money and signed memorabilia to a variety of medical, educational, and societal causes.

After *The Soloist*, he signed on to do another action movie—director Guy Ritchie's modern retelling of *Sherlock Holmes*. Downey played the lead character as part sleuth, part action hero. Jude Law starred opposite him as Dr. Watson. Downey's wife produced the film. When *Sherlock Holmes* was released in 2009, it set Christmas box office records, bringing in nearly $25 million on its first day in theaters.

Sherlock Holmes proved to be a grueling shoot. One fight scene sent Downey to the hospital to stitch up a cut on his lip. When the film was released, Downey found himself with another Golden Globe win. During his acceptance speech, Downey acknowledged his wife's influence on his career. "I really don't want to thank my wife because I could be bussing tables at the Daily Grill right now if not for her," he joked.[6]

||||||||||||||||||||||||||||||||||||||||||||||||||||||||||||||||||||

CASTING INTO THE FUTURE

In 2011, Downey and his wife were living on a seven-acre (3-ha), $13 million horse ranch in Malibu. Downey was hard at work on sequels to *Iron Man* and *Sherlock Holmes*, as well as a new superhero movie, *The Avengers*, in which he would again star as his Iron Man character, Tony Stark. He was earning an estimated $25 million per movie.

WORKING COUPLE ||||||||||||||||||||||||||||||||||||||||||||||||||||||||||||||||||||

Downey and Levin met while working on *Gothika*, and their working relationship didn't end there. The couple started their own production company, called Team Downey, to produce films for Warner Brothers studios. One of the first projects Team Downey signed on to produce was *Yucatan*, a movie about a team of thieves trying to track down buried treasure in Mexico.

Being together at home and at work hasn't put a damper on Downey's marriage. In fact, the opposite is true. "We love working together," Downey said. "Making movies is so energy- and time-consuming that it takes you away from your real life for big chunks of time. So I get to escape *with* her, as opposed to *from* her."[7]

He and Susan started their own production company with Warner Bros., called Team Downey. Downey had his handprints and footprints immortalized in cement alongside the other celebrity prints lining Grauman's Chinese Theatre in Los Angeles.

Downey had been off drugs for more than seven years. He had a good relationship with his 17-year-old son, Indio, and a solid marriage with Susan. In August 2011, the couple announced they were expecting their first child together in early 2012.

At age 46, Downey realized just how far he had come—and how close to the edge he'd once gotten. He knew that he could never go back to being the self-destructive guy in the orange prison jumpsuit again. "I took my life to the 11th hour and the 59th minute," he said. "Luckily, the clock didn't strike midnight, and I didn't turn into a pumpkin."[8]

||||||||||

Downey attended the premiere of *Iron Man 2* in 2010. By 2011, he was working on another sequel in the successful franchise, *Iron Man 3*.

TIMELINE

1965

1970

1983

Robert Downey Jr. is born on April 4.

Downey acts in his first movie—his father's film *Pound*.

Downey lands a role in the John Sayles movie *Baby It's You*.

1987

1987

1987

Downey gets his first starring movie role, appearing in *The Pick-Up Artist* with Molly Ringwald.

Downey stars in *Less Than Zero*, a role that mirrors his life.

Downey checks himself into drug rehabilitation for the first time.

1984	1985	1985

Downey begins dating Sarah Jessica Parker.	Downey appears in the movie *Weird Science* with Anthony Michael Hall.	Downey is hired as a regular cast member on *Saturday Night Live*.

1990	1992	1992

Downey stars in *Air America* with Mel Gibson.	Downey stars in Sir Richard Attenborough's film *Chaplin* and is nominated for an Academy Award.	Downey marries actress/singer Deborah Falconer on May 29.

TIMELINE

1993

Downey's son, Indio, is born on September 7.

1996

Downey is arrested on June 23.

1996

On July 16, Downey wanders into neighbor Lisa Curtis's house and falls asleep in her son's bed in what becomes known as the "Goldilocks" incident.

2000

On November 25, Downey is arrested for drug possession at the Merv Griffin Resort Hotel in Palm Springs, California.

2004

On April 26, Falconer and Downey's divorce is finalized.

2004

Downey releases his first music album, *The Futurist*.

1997	1999	1999
On December 8, Downey is sentenced to 180 days at the Los Angeles County Jail for violating his parole.	On February 11, Downey is sentenced to three years in state prison for violating probation from his 1996 drug conviction.	In August, Downey is sent to the California Substance Abuse Treatment Facility. 

2005	2008	2009
Downey and Susan Levin marry at an estate in the Hamptons on August 27.	Downey stars in *Iron Man*. 	Downey stars in *Sherlock Holmes*, a role that earns him a Golden Globe.

FULL NAME

Robert John Downey Jr.

DATE OF BIRTH

April 4, 1965

PLACE OF BIRTH

New York (Greenwich Village), New York

MARRIAGE

Deborah Falconer (May 29, 1992)

Susan Levin (August 27, 2005)

CHILDREN

Indio Falconer Downey

SELECTED FILMS AND TELEVISION APPEARANCES

Pound (1970), *Weird Science* (1985), *Chaplin* (1992), *Ally McBeal* (2000–2002), *The Singing Detective* (2003), *Iron Man* (2008), *Tropic Thunder* (2008), *Sherlock Holmes* (2009), *Iron Man 2* (2010), *Sherlock Holmes: A Game of Shadows* (2011)

SELECTED AWARDS

- Nominated for the 1993 Academy Award for Best Actor in a Leading Role for *Chaplin* (1992)
- Won the 2001 Golden Globe for Best Performance by an Actor in a Supporting Role in a Series, Mini-Series or Motion Picture Made for TV for *Ally McBeal*
- Nominated for the 2009 Academy Award for Best Performance by an Actor in a Supporting Role for *Tropic Thunder* (2008)
- Won the 2010 Golden Globe for Best Performance by an Actor in a Motion Picture—Musical or Comedy for *Sherlock Holmes* (2009)

PHILANTHROPY

Downey's favorite cause is reforming prisons and improving rehabilitation for former prisoners. He gives widely to charities and social causes.

> **"I took my life to the 11th hour and the 59th minute. Luckily, the clock didn't strike midnight, and I didn't turn into a pumpkin."**
>
> *—ROBERT DOWNEY JR.*

GLOSSARY

avant-garde—Something that is unusual or experimental.

disfigured—Injured or damaged so that it does not look as attractive.

domestic—Having to do with a family that lives together.

GED—High school equivalency credential.

idealistic—Basing one's life on ideas or theories, instead of facts and reality.

improvisation—The act of making up an acting scene or comedy skit on the spot, instead of working from a script and rehearsing.

incarceration—The state of being in prison.

mannerism—A person's particular way of speaking, moving, or behaving.

mystique—A sense of mystery or wonder that surrounds a person.

nuptials—A wedding or marriage.

parole—A release from prison depending on the prisoner's continued good behavior.

probation—A release from prison for good behavior, during which time the person is carefully supervised.

rehabilitation—A type of program that helps people get over drugs, alcohol, or a serious injury.

reincarnation—The return of a person's soul after death in another body.

resurgence—Becoming popular or prominent once again.

satirical—The use of wit or sarcasm to poke fun at human errors.

tepid—Lacking in conviction or real interest.

uninhibited—Free from restraint; not worried about what other people think.

ADDITIONAL RESOURCES

SELECTED BIBLIOGRAPHY

Caro, Mark. "A Sobering Journey: Robert Downey Jr. Zigzags His Way Back to Desirability." *Chicago Tribune*. Chicago Tribune, 16 Nov. 2003. Web. 2 Aug. 2011.

"Encore Presentation: Robert Downey Jr.'s Life of Talent and Trouble." *CNN.com*. CNN, 14 July 2001. Web. 13 Sept. 2011.

Falk, Ben. *Robert Downey Jr.: The Fall and Rise of the Comeback Kid*. London: Portico, 2010. Print.

France, David, and John Horn. "Robert Downey Jr. Takes One Day at a Time." *Newsweek*. 12 Feb. 2001: 52-54. Print.

Howden, Martin. *Robert Downey Jr.: The Biography*. London: John Blake, 2010. Print.

FURTHER READINGS

Fleischman, Sid. *Sir Charlie: Chaplin, the Funniest Man in the World*. New York: Greenwillow, 2010. Print.

Manning, Matthew. *Iron Man: The Ultimate Guide to the Armored Super Hero*. New York: DK, 2010. Print.

WEB SITES

To learn more about Robert Downey Jr., visit ABDO Publishing Company online at **www.abdopublishing.com**. Web sites about Robert Downey Jr. are featured on our Book Links page. These links are routinely monitored and updated to provide the most current information available.

PLACES TO VISIT

London Film Museum
County Hall, Riverside Building, South Bank, London SE1
020-7202-7040
http://www.londonfilmmuseum.com
The London Film Museum features collections of movie
props and costumes. Its exhibits include a tribute
to Charlie Chaplin.

Museum of Comic and Cartoon Art
594 Broadway, Suite 401, New York, NY 10012
212-254-3511
http://www.moccany.org/
The Museum of Comic and Cartoon Art features exhibits
on the history of cartoons and comics, including Marvel
Comics characters such as Iron Man.

The Studios at Paramount
5555 Melrose Avenue, Hollywood, CA 90038
323-956-1777
http://www.paramountstudios.com/special-events/tours.
html
Iron Man production company Paramount is the longest
operating movie studio in Hollywood. It offers tours of its
back lot, where participants can see sets and locations from
movie history.

SOURCE NOTES

CHAPTER 1. THE MAKING OF A SUPERHERO

1. "Robert Downey Jr.: Why Is He Famous." *Askmen.com*. IGN Entertainment, n.d. Web. 26 Aug. 2011.

2. Lucy O'Loughlin. "Robert Downey Jr.'s Heroic Comeback." *The List*. The List, 2 May 2008. Web. 2 Aug. 2011.

3. "Robert Downey Jr." *Inside the Actor's Studio*. Bravo, 9 Jul. 2006. Television.

4. Rachel Abramowitz. "From Zero to Hero." *Los Angeles Times*. Los Angeles Times, 27 Apr. 2008. Web. 2 Aug. 2011.

5. Peter Bradshaw. "Film Reviews: Iron Man 2." *The Guardian* 30 Apr. 2010. *ProQuest*. Web. 10 Oct. 2011.

CHAPTER 2. AN UNCONVENTIONAL CHILDHOOD

1. Daisy Fried. "Senior Class." *Philadelphia City Paper*. Philadelphia City Paper, 24 Apr.–1 May 1997. Web. 2 Aug. 2011.

2. "Robert Downey Jr." *Inside the Actor's Studio*. Bravo, 9 Jul. 2006. Television.

3. Ben Falk. *Robert Downey Jr.: The Fall and Rise of the Comeback Kid*. London: Portico, 2010. Print. 27.

4. Ibid. 31.

CHAPTER 3. MAKING IT AS AN ACTOR

1. Mike Figgis. *Projections 10: Hollywood Film-Makers on Film-Making*. London: Faber & Faber, 2000. *Robert Downey Jr. Film Guide*. Web. 10 Oct. 2011.

2. Martin Howden. *Robert Downey Jr.: The Biography*. London: John Blake, 2010. Print. 12.

3. Ben Falk. *Robert Downey Jr.: The Fall and Rise of the Comeback Kid*. London: Portico, 2010. Print. 34

4. "Robert Downey Jr." *Inside the Actor's Studio*. Bravo, 9 Jul. 2006. Television.

5. Roger Ebert. "Two Girls and a Guy." *Suntimes.com*. Chicago Sun-Times, 24 Apr. 1998. Web. 6 Sept. 2011.

CHAPTER 4. DEEP INTO DRUGS

1. David Smith. "The Star Who Came Back from the Depths." *Guardian*. Guardian News and Media, 23 Aug. 2008. Web. 2 Aug. 2011.

2. "Robert Downey Jr." *Inside the Actor's Studio*. Bravo, 9 Jul. 2006. Television.

3. Lowri Williams. "Sarah Jessica Parker Knows All About Addiction." *Entertainmentwise.com*. Entertainmentwise, 15 March 2006. Web. 2 Aug. 2011.

4. Ben Falk. *Robert Downey Jr.: The Fall and Rise of the Comeback Kid.* London: Portico, 2010. Print. 58.

5. Ibid. 56.

6. Jamie Diamond. "Robert Downey Jr. Is Chaplin (on Screen) and a Child (Off)." *New York Times*. New York Times, 20 Dec. 1992. Web. 2 Aug. 2011.

7. Phoebe Hoban. "How Robert Downey Jr. Is Coping with Prison." *Us Weekly* 19 Jun. 2000: 30–31. Print.

8. Ben Falk. *Robert Downey Jr.: The Fall and Rise of the Comeback Kid.* London: Portico, 2010. Print. 65.

CHAPTER 5. BAD CHOICES

1. Caryn James. "Corruption on Campus, In 'Johnny Be Good.'" *New York Times*. New York Times, 25 Mar. 1988. Web. 8 Sept. 2011.

2. Martin Howden. *Robert Downey Jr.: The Biography*. London: John Blake, 2010. Print. 81.

3. "Air America." *The Robert Downey Jr. Film Guide*. Dandychick.com, n.d. Web. 8 Sept. 2011.

4. Gioia Diliberto. "Scarcely Out of Their Teens, Sarah Parker and Robert Downey Play House in Hollywood." *People*. Time Inc., 30 Sept. 1985. Web. 2 Aug. 2011.

5. Ben Falk. *Robert Downey Jr.: The Fall and Rise of the Comeback Kid.* London: Portico, 2010. Print. 65.

6. Martin Howden. *Robert Downey Jr.: The Biography*. London: John Blake, 2010. Print. 97.

7. Ibid. 97.

8. Katherine Thomson. "Robert Downey Jr. on Dating Sarah Jessica Parker, Parenting, and Drug Use." *Huff Post Entertainment*. TheHuffingtonPost.com, 16 Apr. 2008. Web. 2 Aug. 2011.

CHAPTER 6. BECOMING CHAPLIN

1. Ben Falk. *Robert Downey Jr.: The Fall and Rise of the Comeback Kid.* London: Portico, 2010. Print. 75.

2. Vincent Canby. "Chaplin (1992)." *New York Times*. New York Times, 25 Dec. 1992. Web. 12 Sept. 2011.

3. Ben Falk. *Robert Downey Jr.: The Fall and Rise of the Comeback Kid.* London: Portico, 2010. Print. 110.

4. "Biography for Robert Downey Jr." *IMDb.com*. IMDb.com, n.d. Web. 12 Sept. 2011.

5. Owen Gleiberman. "Hugo Pool (1997)." *Entertainment Weekly*. Entertainment Weekly, 12 Dec. 1997. Web. 12 Sept. 2011.

6. "Downey Jr. Hoping His Jinx Stops Here." *Orlando Sentinel*. Orlando Sentinel, 26 Jan. 1996. Web. 12 Sept. 2011.

CHAPTER 7. TROUBLE WITH THE LAW

1. "Biography for Robert Downey Jr." *IMDb.com*. IMDb.com, n.d. Web. 12 Sept. 2011.

2. George Rush and Joanna Molloy. "Downey's Inside Pitch." *Nydailynews.com*. NY Daily News, 19 Aug. 1999. Web. 2 Aug. 2011.

3. Mick LaSalle. "The End of Downey's Greatness?" *SFgate.com*. Hearst Newspapers, 7 May 2010. Web. 13 Sept. 2011.

4. George Rush and Joanna Molloy. "It's Back Behind Bars for Downey." *Nydailynews.com*. NY Daily News, 6 Aug. 1999. Web. 13 Sept. 2011.

5. Ibid.

6. "Robert Downey Jr." *Inside the Actor's Studio*. Bravo, 9 Jul. 2006. Television.

7. Shauna Snow. "Arts and Entertainment Reports." *Los Angeles Times*. Los Angeles Times, 14 Sept. 2000. Web. 12 Sept. 2011.

8. Ben Falk. *Robert Downey Jr.: The Fall and Rise of the Comeback Kid*. London: Portico, 2010. Print. 158.

9. Dan Snierson. "The Ups and Downs of 'Ally McBeal.'" *Entertainment Weekly*. Entertainment Weekly, 3 Nov. 2000. Web. 12 Sept. 2011.

10. Steve Vineberg. "Delivering Something Real to 'Ally McBeal.'" *New York Times*. New York Times, 18 Mar. 2001. Web. 14 Sept. 2011.

11. John Horn. "Robert Downey Jr. Takes One Day at a Time." *Newsweek*. Newsweek/DailyBeast, 11 Feb. 2001. Web. 14 Sept. 2011.

12. George Rush and Joanna Molloy. "Elton to Downey: This Is Your Song." *Nydailynews.com*. NY Daily News, 22 Aug. 2001. Web. 14 Sept. 2011.

CHAPTER 8. EMERGING FROM THE DARKNESS

1. Barry Knowlton. "Robert Downey Jr. on the Upswing." *The Post and Courier (Charleston, SC)* 19 Oct. 2003. *Google News*. Web. 14 Sept. 2011.

2. Anthony Benigno. "Robert Downey Jr. on 'Today Show': Actor Opens Up about Friendships with Charlie Sheen, Mel Gibson." *Nydailynews.com.* NY Daily News, 2 Nov 2010. Web. 14 Sept. 2011.

3. "Halle Berry—Interviews." *TalkTalk.co.uk.* Talk Talk, n.d. Web. 14 Sept. 2011.

4. Katherine Thomson. "Robert Downey Jr. on Dating Sarah Jessica Parker, Parenting, and Drug Use." *Huff Post Entertainment.* TheHuffingtonPost.com, 16 Apr. 2008. Web. 2 Aug. 2011.

5. Samantha Booth. "Robert Downey Jr. Admits: "I Won't Forget My Time in the Gutter." *Dailyrecord.co.uk.* Scottish Daily Record, 10 Apr. 2008. Web. 14 Sept. 2011.

6. Kevin West. "Robert Downey Jr.? Call Him Mr. Clean." *Wmagazine.* Condé Nast, Mar. 2007. Web. 15 Sept. 2011.

7. Ben Falk. *Robert Downey Jr.: The Fall and Rise of the Comeback Kid.* London: Portico, 2010. Print. 207.

CHAPTER 9. RECOVERY, REINVENTION, AND CAREER REBIRTH

1. "Downey but Not Yet Out." *Sundaysun.co.uk.* Sunday Sun, 18 Aug. 2006. Web. 15 Sept. 2011.

2. Nicholas Fonseca. "The Futurist (2004)." *Entertainment Weekly.* Entertainment Weekly, 26 Nov. 2004. Web. 15 Sept. 2011.

3. John Aizlewood. "A 'Great Music Talent.'" *London Evening Standard.* ES London, 29 Apr. 2005. Web. 15 Sept. 2011.

4. Richard Corliss. "Robert Downey Jr., *Iron Man.*" *Time.* Time, 17 Dec. 2008. Web. 1 Oct. 2011.

5. Erik Hedegaard. "The Man Who Wasn't There." *Rolling Stone* 21 Aug. 2008. *EBSCO Megafile.* Web. 14 Oct. 2011.

6. "Robert Downey Jr.—Golden Globe Awards—Best Actor." *YouTube.* YouTube, 10 May 2011. Web. 10 Oct. 2011.

7. Mickey McMonagle. "New Sherlock Holmes Film Star Robert Downey Jr. on His Return to the A-list from Booze and Jail Hell." *Dailyrecord.co.uk.* Scottish Daily Record, 26 Dec. 2009. Web. 15 Sept. 2011.

8. Barry Koltnow. "Robert Downey Jr. Is Keeping His Nose to the Grindstone." *The Star Online.* Star Publications, 31 Oct. 2005. Web. 2 Aug. 2011.

INDEX

Air America, 42, 65, 79
Ally McBeal, 71–73, 75, 88
America's Sweethearts, 73, 75
Attenborough, Sir Richard,
   49–51, 53, 56
Avengers, The, 93

Baby It's You, 25–26
Black and White, 67, 70
Brat Pack, 27–29
Broderick, Matthew, 42, 45

Chances Are, 40–41
Chaplin, 11, 49–51, 53–55,
   58
Chaplin, Charlie, 9, 28,
   50–51
Curtis, Lisa, 62

*Downey, Allyson, 16–18, 24
Downey, Indio, 47, 69, 75,
   84, 94
Downey Jr., Robert
   arrests, 9, 64, 74, 77
   awards, 9, 54, 73, 91–92
   childhood, 15–19
   divorce, 12, 75, 80
   early career, 23–25
   education, 18–21, 23, 70
   family, 15–19, 21, 24–25,
      33, 43–45, 47, 69, 75,
      83, 92–94
   jail time, 64–65, 68–69

music, 88–89
   poetry, 44
Downey Sr., Robert, 16–18,
   21, 24–25, 33, 44
drug abuse, 9, 12, 33–37,
   39, 44–45, 47, 55,
   62–65, 67, 73–75, 78

*Ernst, Laura, 43–44
Exodus Recovery Center,
   63–64

*Falconer, Deborah, 45, 47,
   69, 75, 80
Favreau, Jon, 8, 10–11
Ford, Elsie, 16, 18
Foster, Jodie, 56
Futurist, The, 88–89

*Gibson, Mel, 42, 73, 79
"Goldilocks" incident,
   62–63
Good Night and Good Luck,
   83
Gothika, 80, 93
Greenwich Village, New
   York City, 17, 19

*Hoffman, Abbie, 17
Home for the Holidays, 56

Iron Man, 8, 12, 89–90, 93

*John, Elton, 74
Johnny Be Good, 39–40

Kanievska, Marek, 35
Kelley, David E., 71
Kiss Kiss Bang Bang, 9, 83, 84

Less Than Zero, 31, 35, 36
Levin, Susan, 80–81, 83, 93
London, England, 18, 42, 54
Los Angeles, 18–19, 42–43, 44, 47, 61, 64, 70, 94

Maisel, David, 12
Marvel Studios, 7, 12, 90

1969, 40

One Night Stand, 58
Only You, 55

Parker, Sarah Jessica, 26, 28, 34, 44–45
Pick-Up Artist, The, 30–31, 35, 65
Pound, 17, 24
Putney Swope, 16, 18

rehab, 9, 36–37, 63, 68, 70–71, 77, 78
Rented Lips, 39–40
Restoration, 56

Santa Monica High School, 19–21
Saturday Night Live, 29–30
Scanner Darkly, A, 83
Shapiro, Robert, 67
Sherlock Holmes, 92–93
Sierra Tucson, 37
Singing Detective, The, 9, 79
Soloist, The, 91–92

Team Downey, 93, 94
Toback, James, 30, 65
Tomei, Marisa, 55
Tropic Thunder, 90–91
True Believer, 40
Tuff Turf, 28
Two Girls and a Guy, 65–66, 88

U.S. Marshals, 65

Walden House, 70
Weird Science, 28–29
Wonder Boys, 67

ABOUT THE AUTHOR

Stephanie Watson is a freelance writer based in Atlanta, Georgia. Over her 20-plus-year career, she has written for television, radio, the Web, and print. Watson has authored more than two-dozen books, including, *Celebrity Biographies: Daniel Radcliffe*, *Heath Ledger: Talented Actor*, and *Anderson Cooper: Profile of a TV Journalist*.

PHOTO CREDITS